MILL GIRLS
OF
LOWELL

JEFF LEVINSON

 Perspectives on History

D1491252

⊕ **History**Compass

Boston, Massachusetts

HistoryCompass
www.historycompass.com

ISBN 978-1-932663-15-0 paperback edition

Printed in the United States of America

Cover Images:

Merrimack Mills and boarding houses in 1848 and
Winslow Homer's *The Bobbin Girl*, 1871.

Library of Congress Cataloging-in-Publication Data

Mill girls of Lowell / edited by Jeff Levinson.
    p. cm. -- (Perspectives on history)
ISBN 1-932663-15-0
1. Women textile workers--Massachusetts--Lowell--History. [1. Textile industry--Massachusetts--Lowell.] I. Levinson, Jeff, 1963-
  HD6073.T42U555 2007
  331.4'877097444--dc22
  2006103354

‌Table of Contents‌

Introduction

The growing textile industry in Lowell, Massachusetts wove together strands of modernization in pre-Civil War America. Lowell embodied the American industrial revolution, beginning the shift from farm to factory, from rural to urban. Technological innovation was coupled with the plentiful power supply harnessed from the Merrimack River, with sufficient capital formed by wealthy entrepreneurs, with new methods of industrial organization and management, and, most important, with labor provided by "mill girls."

Textile manufacturing was moving away from piecework sent out to individual workers. By the early 19th century, the textile industry in New England was growing, and it needed workers to run the looms in larger-scale factories. It found those workers first in children and the mill girls, women who moved from New England farmhouses to Lowell boardinghouses to work in the booming textile mills. For many of these women, they were independent for the first time. They lived on their own, earned their own money, and paid their own rent. They also started to recognize the power of their numbers and formed early labor organizations. One mill worker, Sarah Bagley, became an active labor organizer, agitating for reform. Other mill workers like Lucy Larcom and Harriet Hanson Robinson wrote articles and poems for the "Lowell

Offering," a magazine written by female mill workers from 1840 through 1845, a record that gives us a glimpse of their lives in the mills and boardinghouses.

Immigrants gradually replaced the mill girls as the main source of labor for the Lowell mills. In turn, falling prices for cloth and greater competition led to the textile industry's decline in New England as companies moved to lower wage areas like the American South to remain competitive. After World War I, little textile manufacturing remained in Lowell from its industrial heyday.

The Merrimack River runs out of the mountains of
New Hampshire south into Massachusetts, over Pawtucket
Falls, past the city of Lowell, and into the Atlantic Ocean
at Newburyport, Massachusetts.

In 1822, canals were constructed at the Pawtucket
Falls at Lowell to channel the fast-moving water and take
advantage of this natural power source. One year later, the
first textile mills opened, producing cotton cloth that was
shipped worldwide. Between 1825 and 1847 other canals
were built. A city and an industry grew. Lowell's population
increased from 2,500 in 1826 to 33,000 in 1850 to 78,000 in
1890.[1] Lowell mills produced 750,000 yards of cotton cloth

[1] Sources for population, mill production, and employment include Arthur L.Eno, Jr., ed.,
Cotton Was King (New Hampshire Publishing Company in collaboration with the Lowell
Historical Society, 1976), Appendix A; Center for Lowell History, U. Mass. Lowell,
"Primary Sources of Lowell," April 2006, http://library.uml.edu/clh/index.html. Other
useful sources for an overview of Lowell's textile manufacturing industry and the mill
girls include the U.S. National Park Service, Lowell National Historical Park and Tsongas
Industrial History Center, at http://www.nps.gov/lowe/home.htm; Thomas Dublin,
Women at Work (New York, Columbia University Press, 1979); and Harriet H.
Robinson, *Loom and Spindle* (1898; reprinted: Hawaii: Press Pacifica, 1976).

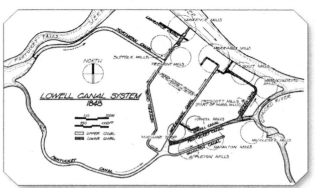

*Lowell Canal System as of 1848, from 1975 survey by the Office of Archeology
and Historic Preservation under direction of National Park Service.*

a week in 1835, 2.2 million in 1855, and 4.7 million in 1888. From 22 mills and 5,000 women employed in 1835 to 175 mills and 13,000 women employed in 1888, Lowell had become the United States' largest industrial center, "stretching far and wide its chaos of brick masonry," as poet John Greenleaf Whittier put it.

TEXTILE INDUSTRY

New England textile mills processed raw cotton shipped from the South. The Lowell mills cleaned, carded (aligned the fibers), spun, and wove the cotton into cloth that was then shipped all over the world. The invention of a new technology in the previous generation – the cotton gin – led to an explosion of cotton production. Southern cotton generated huge profits for the plantation owners. It also made them rely more and more on slaves to work the cotton plantations. Northern textile mills used Southern cotton to feed the looms.

Boott Cotton Mills, circa 1850 (courtesy Lowell National Historic Park, illustrator Kirk Doggett)

In the late 1700s, Slater's Mill on the Blackstone River in Rhode Island represented early efforts to develop larger-scale, water-powered, centralized textile manufacture in the United States, but the weaving was still sent to workers' homes to be finished. Later mills (around 1815) on the Charles River in Waltham, Massachusetts, built by Francis Cabot Lowell and other entrepreneurs from Boston, were much larger, housed all the textile manufacturing in one place, and used power looms recreated from English designs. The mills also began employing a new kind of worker: young women from the country. Within 15 years, new factory designs, such as those at Lowell, Massachusetts, expanded on the Waltham architecture, with large four or five story mills. Through this system, cloth production boomed, and mill owners earned huge profits.

THE MILL GIRLS

Hiring young women from the country grew from an experiment in Waltham to a massive industrial organization in Lowell. The young (ages about 15-25) mill girls left the farms and rural areas of New England for better opportunities in the city. They worked up to 13 hour days in the factories, under regimented schedules and strict rules of behavior outside the working day. The mill girls were also, for one of the first times on such a scale, able to live independently, earn their own money, and make choices about where they lived and what they would do. They were part of a society of other women who had come from similar circumstances. When they left the mills, to return home, move out West, get married, or get another job, the women would receive an "honorable discharge," evidencing their work and their independence.

Harriet Hanson Robinson, writing 60 years after she began work at age 11 in Lowell in 1835, described the mill workers in the early days:

At the time the Lowell cotton-mills were started, the factory girl was the lowest among women. In England and in France particularly, great injustice had been done to her real character; she was represented as subjected to influences that could not fail to destroy her purity and self-respect. In the eyes of her overseer she was but a brute, a slave, to be beaten, pinched, and pushed about. It was to overcome this prejudice that such high wages had been offered to women [by the Lowell mill owners] that they might be induced to become mill-girls, in spite of the opprobrium that still clung to this "degrading occupation." At first only a few came; for, though tempted by the high wages to be regularly paid in "cash," there were many who still preferred to go on working at some more *genteel* employment at seventy-five cents a week and their board.

But in a short time the prejudice against factory labor wore away, and the Lowell mills became filled with blooming and energetic New England women. They were naturally intelligent, had mother-wit, and fell easily into the ways of their new life. They soon began to associate with those who formed the community in which they had come to live, and were invited to their houses. They went to the same church, and sometimes married into some of the best families. Or if they returned to their secluded homes again, instead of being looked down upon as "factory girls" by the squire's or the lawyer's family, they were more often welcomed as coming from the metropolis, bringing new fashions, new books, and new ideas with them.

Source: Harriet H. Robinson, *Loom and Spindle* (1898) (reprinted Hawaii: Press Pacifica, 1976), pp. 41-42.

HOUSING AND COMMUNITY

The mill girls lived in groups of 25 to 40, sometimes more, in company-managed boardinghouses, for which they paid about $5 a month in the 1830s. In some ways, boardinghouses mirrored the regimentation of the factories. Mealtimes and curfews were set, and boardinghouse keepers were supposed to report violations of the rules to the women's employers. Yet the boarders formed close communities among themselves. They shared rooms and meals. New hires learned from the older women and conformed to urban norms and a high moral code of conduct. On their own time, they wrote letters, read, sewed, talked, and played piano. They became friends and supported each other, including in their later efforts to improve working conditions. They read and discussed newspapers, magazines, the Bible, literature, and other books. They attended church regularly. They went to lectures and on walks.

Mill worker Lucy Larcom wrote in her memoir about the intellectual environment of Lowell:

> Everything that was new or strange came to us at Lowell. And most of the remarkable people of the day came also....
>
> ...Many of the prominent men of the country were in the habit of giving Lyceum lectures, and the Lyceum lecture of that day was a means of education, conveying to the people the results of study and thought through the best minds. At Lowell it was more patronized by the mill-people than any mere entertainment. We had John Quincy Adams, Edward Everett, John Pierpont, and Ralph Waldo Emerson among our lecturers, with numerous distinguished clergymen of the day. Daniel Webster was once in the city, trying a law case. Some of my girl friends went to the court-room and had a glimpse of his face, but I just missed seeing him.
>
> Source: Lucy Larcom, *A New England Girlhood* (1889) (reprinted, Gloucester, MA, 1973), pp. 252-53.

TECHNOLOGY AND INNOVATION

Some technology to run the mills was created in Lowell and other parts of the United States. Some was copied from English designs.

Samuel Slater's success at his mill on the Blackstone River in Rhode Island was made possible by Slater's having copied a power "water frame" for spinning, which he learned of during his time in England supervising a factory. Francis Cabot Lowell visited England in the early 1800s and, with the help of master mechanic Paul Moody, copied the design for the English power loom he had seen. Other industrial innovations of this period included a more efficient turbine for converting water flow into power and later conversion to more dependable steam power. Machine shops associated with the factories further improved the equipment. America was developing skilled machinists and master mechanics.

CANALS

The Pawtucket Canal on the Merrimack River was built to allow timber to be floated to the port city of Newburyport, for shipbuilding. In 1821, a company formed by Boston businessmen began to expand the canal system around Lowell to power new textile mills. By 1850, nearly six miles of canals powered many mills. The canals allowed the factories to harness water and power the machinery. Cheap and plentiful power was critical to the growth of large-scale industry. Constructing the canals also changed the river. Some fish disappeared: salmon, shad, and alewives. Factories polluted the water with trash and dyes.

LABOR

As the textile industry became more industrialized, the mill girls began collectively protesting against working conditions and wage reductions.

One of the first large-scale strikes took place in 1836 against a proposed increase in room and board rates, effectively a 15% wage reduction. (Other, smaller strikes had taken place at mills in the previous decade.) The women – estimated at as many as 2,000, or about one-fourth of the workforce – "turned out," or walked out on strike in protest. The mills shut down. The women believed that they

After the Civil War many cotton mills opened in the South, competing with those in Lowell and other New England areas. (Photo by Lewis Hine, Library of Congress)

were fighting for their independence and dignity. While the women eventually returned to work and did not succeed in fully stopping the room and board rate increase, they had learned how to organize and lead, learned effective tactics for pressuring employers, and won a small victory of keeping the mills' partial payments of their room and board.

The women turned their new-found power to labor reform. In the 1840s, women fought for the 10 hour work day. As part of this reform campaign, Sarah Bagley became one of the leaders. She founded the Lowell Female Labor Reform Association in 1845. She published and edited, with others, the labor newspaper, *Voice of Industry,* to support the "Ten Hour Movement."

INDUSTRIAL DECLINE

Throughout the 19th century, Lowell's textile production increased, but as time went on, employment of immigrants willing to work for lower wages led to a decline in the employment of mill girls. Also, more modern factories outside of Lowell were producing cloth and cutting into the Lowell mills' market. In the South, lower wages, available land, and less government intervention attracted textile manufacturing. After World War I, many of the textile manufacturing companies closed or moved out of Lowell. During the Depression, there were 8,000 textile workers in Lowell, about the number there were 100 years before.

Women and Work

Harriet Robinson (1824-1911) began work in a Lowell textile mill in 1835 and continued there until 1848. In her memoir, Loom and Spindle *(1898), she wrote of the status of women before 1840 and the effects of employment at the mills:*

It must be remembered that at this date woman [sic] had no property rights. A widow could be left without her share of her husband's (or the family) property, a legal "incumbrance" to his estate. A father could make his will without reference to his daughter's share of the inheritance. He usually left her a home on the farm as long as she remained single. A woman was not supposed to be capable of spending her own or of using other people's money. In Massachusetts, before 1840, a woman could not legally be treasurer of her own sewing-society, unless some man were responsible for her.

The law took no cognizance of woman as a money-spender. She was a ward, an appendage, a relict. Thus it happened, that if a woman did not choose to marry, or, when left a widow, to re-marry, she had no choice but to enter one of the few employments open to her, or to become a burden on the charity of some relative.

In almost every New England home would be found one or more of these women, sometimes welcome, more often unwelcome, and leading joyless, and in many instances unsatisfactory, lives. The cotton-factory was a great opening to these lonely and dependent women. From a condition approaching pauperism they were at once placed above want; they could earn money, and spend it as they pleased; and could gratify their tastes and desires without restraint, and without rendering an account to anybody. At last they had found a place in the universe; they were no longer obliged to finish out their faded lives mere burdens to male relatives. Even the *time* of these women was their own, on Sundays and in the evening after the day's work was done. For the first time in this country woman's labor had a money value. She had become not only an earner and a producer, but also a spender of money, a recognized factor in the political economy of her time. And thus a long upward step in our material civilization was taken; woman had begun to earn and hold her own money, and through its aid had learned to think and to act for herself.

Among the older women who sought this new employment were very many lonely and dependent ones, such as used to be mentioned in old wills as "incumbrances" and "relicts," and to whom a chance of earning money was indeed a new revelation. How well I remember some of these solitary ones! As a child of eleven years, I often made fun of them—for children do not see the pathetic side of human life—and imitated their limp carriage and inelastic gait.

TIME TABLE OF THE LOWELL MILLS,

Arranged to make the working time throughout the year average 11 hours per day.

TO TAKE EFFECT SEPTEMBER 21st, 1853.

The Standard time being that of the meridian of Lowell, as shown by the Regulator Clock of AMOS SANBORN, Post Office Corner, Central Street.

From March 20th to September 19th, inclusive.

COMMENCE WORK, at 6.30 A. M. LEAVE OFF WORK, at 6.30 P. M., except on Saturday Evenings. BREAKFAST at 6 A. M. DINNER, at 12 M. Commence Work, after dinner, 12.45 P. M.

From September 20th to March 19th, inclusive.

COMMENCE WORK at 7.00 A. M. LEAVE OFF WORK, at 7.00 P. M., except on Saturday Evenings. BREAKFAST at 6.30 A. M. DINNER, at 12.30 P.M. Commence Work, after dinner, 1.15 P. M.

BELLS.

From March 20th to September 19th, inclusive.

Morning Bells.	Dinner Bells.	Evening Bells.
First bell,............4.30 A. M.	Ring out,..............12.00 M.	Ring out,............6.30 P. M.
Second, 5.30 A. M.; Third, 6.20.	Ring in,............12.35 P. M.	Except on Saturday Evenings.

From September 20th to March 19th, inclusive.

Morning Bells.	Dinner Bells.	Evening Bells.
First bell,............5.00 A. M.	Ring out,............12.30 P. M.	Ring out at..........7.00 P. M.
Second, 6.00 A. M.; Third, 6.50.	Ring in,............1.05 P. M.	Except on Saturday Evenings.

SATURDAY EVENING BELLS.

During APRIL, MAY, JUNE, JULY, and AUGUST, Ring Out, at 6.00 P. M.
The remaining Saturday Evenings in the year, ring out as follows:

SEPTEMBER.	NOVEMBER.	JANUARY.
First Saturday, ring out 6.00 P. M.	Third Saturday ring out 4.00 P. M.	Third Saturday, ring out 4.25 P. M.
Second " " 5.45 "	Fourth " " 3.55 "	Fourth " " 4.35 "
Third " " 5.30 "		
Fourth " " 5.20 "	DECEMBER.	FEBRUARY.
	First Saturday, ring out 3.50 P. M.	First Saturday, ring out 4.45 P. M.
OCTOBER.	Second " " 3.55 "	Second " " 4.55 "
First Saturday, ring out 5.05 P. M.	Third " " 3.55 "	Third " " 5.00 "
Second " " 4.55 "	Fourth " " 4.00 "	Fourth " " 5.10 "
Third " " 4.45 "	Fifth " " 4.00 "	
Fourth " " 4.35 "		MARCH.
Fifth " . " 4.25 "	JANUARY.	First Saturday, ring out 5.25 P. M.
	First Saturday, ring out 4.10 P. M.	Second " " 5.30 "
NOVEMBER.	Second " " 4.15 "	Third " " 5.35 "
First Saturday, ring out 4.15 P. M.		Fourth " " 5.45 "
Second " " 4.05 "		

YARD GATES will be opened at the first stroke of the bells for entering or leaving the Mills.

SPEED GATES commence hoisting three minutes before commencing work.

Penhallow, Printer, Wyman's Exchange, 28 Merrimack St.

Timetable of the Lowell Mills

I can see them now, even after sixty years, just as they looked,—depressed, modest, mincing, hardly daring to look one in the face, so shy and sylvan had been their lives. But after the first pay-day came, and they felt the jingle of silver in their pockets, and had begun to feel its mercurial influence, their bowed heads were lifted, their necks seemed braced with steel, they looked you in the face, sang blithely among their looms or frames, and walked with elastic step to and from their work. And when Sunday came, homespun was no longer their only wear; and how sedately gay in their new attire they walked to church, and how proudly they dropped their silver fourpences into the contribution-box! It seemed as if a great hope impelled them,—the harbinger of the new era that was about to dawn for them and for all women-kind.

Source: Robinson, *Loom and Spindle*, pp. 41-42.

Robinson also described the effects of their earnings on the female factory workers and their families:

It may be added here, that the majority of the mill-girls made...good use of their money, so newly earned, and of whose value they had hitherto known so little. They were necessarily industrious. They were also frugal and saving. It was their custom on the first day of every month, after paying their board-bill ($1.25 a week), to put their wages in the savings-bank. There the money stayed, on interest, until they withdrew it, to carry home or to use for a special purpose. It is easy to see how much good this sum would do in a rural community where money, as a means of exchange, had been scarce. Into the barren homes many of them had left it went like a quiet stream, carrying with it beauty and refreshment. The mortgage was lifted from the homestead; the farmhouse was painted; the barn rebuilt; modern improvements (including Mrs. Child's "Frugal Housewife"—the first American cook-book) were introduced into the mother's kitchen, and books and newspapers began to ornament the sitting-room table.

Some of the mill-girls helped maintain widowed mothers, or drunken, incompetent, or invalid fathers. Many of them educated the younger children of the family, and young men were sent to college with the money furnished by the untiring industry of their women relatives.

Indeed, the most prevailing incentive to our labor was to secure the means of education for some *male* member of the family. To make a *gentleman* of a brother or a son, to give him a college education, was the dominant thought in the minds of a great many of these provident mill-girls. I have known more than one to give every cent of her wages, month after month, to her brother, that he might get the education necessary to enter some profession. I have known a mother to work years in this way for her boy.

Source: Robinson, *Loom and Spindle*, pp. 46-47.

The Lowell Offering, August 1845.

The Lowell Offering

The Lowell Offering *was a magazine begun in 1840 for the purpose of publishing the fiction, poems, and essays of the mill girls.*

Lucy Larcom, who began work in Lowell at the age of 11, described the origins of the Lowell Offering:

...my sister Emilie became acquainted with a family of bright girls, near neighbors of ours, who proposed that we should join with them, and form a little society for writing and discussion, to meet fortnightly at their house. We met,—I think I was the youngest of the group,—prepared a Constitution and By-Laws, and named ourselves "The Improvement Circle." If I remember rightly, my sister was our first president. The older ones talked and wrote on many subjects quite above me. I was shrinkingly bashful, as half-grown girls usually are, but I wrote my little essays and read them, and listed to the rest, and enjoyed it all exceedingly. Out of this little "Improvement Circle" grew the larger one whence issued the "Lowell Offering," a year or two later.

Source: Larcom, *A New England Girlhood*, pp. 174-175.

Larcom also wrote about the disbelief with which the Lowell Offering was received from some of its wide readership:

> ...there were those to whom it seemed incredible that a girl could, in the pauses of her work, put together words with her pen that it would do to print; and after a while the assertion was circulated, through some distant newspaper, that our magazine was not written by ourselves at all, but by "Lowell lawyers." This seemed almost too foolish a suggestion to contradict, but the editor of the "Offering" thought it best to give the name and occupation of some of the writers by way of refutation.
>
> Source: Larcom, *A New England Girlhood*, p. 223.

In an editorial published in one of the last volumes of the Lowell Offering, the then-editor, Harriet Farley, gave her view of the purpose served by the Lowell Offering:

> "...the aim of the Offering was a very simple one—simple in itself, though surprising in its results. It was published simply in the words of one of its contributors,
>
>   "to show
> What factory girls had power to do."

It was a collection of compositions, and read and praised for its unexpected literary merit. No particular tone was given to it....One thing, however, might reasonably be expected from their writings— that they would exhibit the state of feeling among the contributors; and it was found that the Offering possessed a cheerful tone. There were, sometimes, in its tales, essays, and poems, allusions to trials, griefs, deprivations, and discomforts. The wearisome hours, the monotonous toil, the separation from friends, and the seclusion from the accustomed healthful and buoyant influences of nature, were spoken of in terms—it might be of regret and sadness, but not of captious dissent. And we rejoiced at this. We thank them that they have presented themselves to their

Boarding house parlor as it would have appeared to the mill girls. (Courtesy Lowell National Historic Park)

REGULATIONS

BOARDING HOUSES

OF THE

MIDDLESEX COMPANY

THE tenants of the Boarding Houses are not to board, or permit any part of their houses to be occupied by any person except those in the employ of the Company.

They will be considered answerable for any improper conduct in their houses, and are not to permit their boarders to have company at unseasonable hours.

The doors must be closed at ten o'clock in the evening, and no one admitted after that time without some reasonable excuse.

The keepers of the Boarding Houses must give an account of the number, names, and employment of their boarders, when required; and report the names of such as are guilty of any improper conduct, or are not in the regular habit of attending public worship.

The buildings and yards about them must be kept clean and in good order, and if they are injured otherwise than from ordinary use, all necessary repairs will be made, and charged to the occupant.

It is indispensable that all persons in the employ of the Middlesex Company should be vaccinated who have not been, as also the families with whom they board; which will be done at the expense of the Company.

SAMUEL LAWRENCE, Agent.

JOEL TAYLOR, PRINTER, Daily Courier Office.

The regulations of the boarding houses were very strict, as the matron of the house took on the responsibilities of absent parents, overseeing the daily lives of the young women who lived there. (Courtesy of the Merrimack Valley Textile Museum, Lowell) readers with cheerfulness and self-respect. They have thus done honor to their heads and hearts. They have shown that their first and absorbing thought was not for an advance of wages or a reduction of labor hours. They have given the impression that they were contented even with their humble lot. They have implied that it was quite as important to be good, as to have good. They have striven for improvement of head and heart before that of situation....

...It was the design of its first editor, that [the Offering] should conflict with but one error; that it should be perfectly free from sectarianism in religion, from party politics, and from the disputed topics of the day, as temperance, slavery, and so forth. Other papers were established for discussion and dissemination of thought upon these subjects, and our efforts were not needed....

Source: *Lowell Offering*, Volume V, November 1845, pp. 263-264.

"A Week in the Mill"

Source: Author unknown, *Lowell Offering*, Volume V, 1845, pp. 217-218.

Much has been said of the factory girl and her employment. By some she has been represented as dwelling in a sort of brick-and-mortar paradise, having little to occupy thought save the weaving of gay and romantic fancies, while the spindle or the wheel flies obediently beneath her glance. Others have deemed her a mere servile drudge, chained to her labor by almost as strong a power as that which holds a bondman in his fetters; and, indeed, some have already given her the title of *"the white slave of the North."* Her real situation approaches neither one nor the other of these extremes. Her occupation is as laborious as that of almost any female who earns her own living, while it has also its sunny spots and its cheerful intervals, which make her hard labor seem comparatively pleasant and easy.

Look at her as she commences her weekly task. The rest of the sabbath has made her heart and her step light, and she is early at her accustomed place, awaiting the starting of the machinery. Every thing having been cleaned and neatly arranged on the Saturday night, she has less to occupy her on Monday than on other days; and you may see her leaning from the window to watch the glitter of the sunrise on the water, or looking away at the distant forests and fields, while memory wanders to her beloved country home; or, it may be that she is conversing with a sister-laborer near; returning at regular intervals to see that her work is in order.

Soon the breakfast bell rings; in a moment the whirling wheels are stopped, and she hastens to join the throng which is pouring through the open gate. At the table she mingles with a various group. Each despatches the meal hurriedly, though not often in silence; and if, as is sometimes the case, the rules of politeness are not punctiliously observed by all, the excuse of some lively country girl would be, "They don't give us time for *manners*."

The short half-hour is soon over; the bell rings again; and now our factory girls feels that she has commenced her day's work in earnest. The time is often apt to drag heavily until the dinner hour arrives. Perhaps some part of the work becomes deranged and stops; the constant friction causes a belt of leather to burst into flames; a stranger visits the room, and scans the features and dress of its inmates inquiringly; and there is little else to break the monotony. The afternoon passes in much the same manner. Now and then she mingles with a knot of busy talkers who have collected to discuss some new occurrence, or holds pleasant converse with some intelligent and agreeable friend, whose acquaintance she has formed since her factory life commenced; but much of the time she is left to her own thoughts. While at her work, the clattering and rumbling around her prevent any other noise from attracting her attention, and she *must think*, or her life would be dull indeed.

Thus the day passes on, and evening comes; the time which she feels to be exclusively her own. How much is done in the three short hours from seven to ten o'clock. She has a new dress to finish; a call to make on some distant corporation; a meeting to attend; there is a lecture or a concert at some one of the public halls, and the attendance will be thin if she and her associates are not present; or, if nothing more imperative demands her time, she takes a stroll through the street or to the river with one of her mates, or sits down at home to peruse a new book. At ten o'clock all is still for the night.

The clang of the early bell awakes her to another day, very nearly the counterpart of the one which preceded it. And so the week rolls on, in the same routine, till Saturday comes. Saturday! the welcome sound! She busies herself to remove every particle of cotton and dust from her frames or looms, cheering herself meanwhile with sweet thoughts of the coming sabbath; and when, at an earlier hour than usual, the mill is stoppped, it looks almost beautiful in its neatness....

The writer is aware that this sketch is an imperfect one. Yet there is very little variety in an operative's life, and little difference between it and any other life of labor. It lies

"half in sunlight—half in shade."

Few would wish to spend a whole life in a factory, and few are discontented who do thus seek a subsistence for a term of months or years.

"The Spirit of Discontent"

by Almira, a Lowell mill girl

Source: Author unknown, *Lowell Offering*, Volume I, 1841, pp. 111-114.

"I will not stay in Lowell any longer; I am determined to give my notice this very day," said Ellen Collins, as the earliest bell was tolling to remind us of the hour for labor.

"Why, what is the matter, Ellen? It seems to me you have dreamed out a new idea! Where do you think of going? and what for?"

"I am going home, where I shall not be obliged to rise so early in the morning, nor be dragged about by the ringing of a bell, nor confined in a close noisy room from morning till night. I will not stay here; I am determined to go home in a fortnight."

Such was our brief morning's conversation.

In the evening, as I sat alone, reading, my companions having gone out to public lectures or social meetings, Ellen entered. I saw that she still wore the same gloomy expression of countenance, which had been manifested in the morning; and I was disposed to remove from her mind the evil influence, by a plain common-sense conversation.

"And so, Ellen," said I, "you think it unpleasant to rise so early in the morning, and, be confined in the noisy mill so many hours during the day. And I think so, too, All this, and much more, is very annoying, no doubt, But we must not forget that there are advantages, as well as disadvantages, in this employment, as in every other. If we expect to find all sun-shine and flowers in any station in life, we shall most surely be disappointed. We are very busily engaged during the day; but then we have the evening to ourselves, with no one to dictate to or control us. I have frequently heard you say that you would not be confined to house-hold duties, and that you disliked the millinery business altogether because you could not have your evenings for leisure. You know that in Lowell we have schools, lectures, and meetings of every description, for moral and intellectual improvement."

"All that is very true," replied Ellen, "but if we were to attend every public institution and every evening school which offers itself for our improvement, we might spend every farthing of our earnings, and even more. Then if sickness should overtake us, what are the probable consequences? Here we are, far from kindred and home; and if we have an empty purse, we shall be destitute of *friends* also.

"I do not think so, Ellen, I believe there is no place where there are so many advantages within the reach of the laboring class of people, as exist here; where there is so much equality, so few aristocratic distinctions, and such good fellowship, as may be found in this community. A person has only to be honest, industrious, and moral, though he may not be worth a dollar; while on the other hand, an immoral person, though he should possess wealth, is not respected."

"As to the morality of the place," returned Ellen, "I have no fault to find. I object to the constant hurry of everything. We cannot have time to eat, drink or sleep; we have only thirty minutes, or at most three quarters of an hour, allowed us to go from our work, partake of our food, and return to the noisy clatter of machinery. Up before day, at the clang of the bell—and out of the mill by the clang of the bell—into the mill, and at work, in obedience to that dingdong of a bell—just as though we were so many living machines. I will give my notice to-morrow: go, I will—I won't stay here and be a white slave."

"Ellen," said I, "do you remember what is said of the bee, that it gathers honey even in a poisonous flower? May we not, in like manner, if our hearts are rightly attuned, find many pleasures connected with our employment? Why is it, then, that you so obstinately look altogether on the dark side of a factory life? I think you thought differently while you were at home, on a visit last summer—for you were glad to come back to the mill, in less than four weeks. Tell me, now—why were you so glad to return to the ringing of the bell, the clatter of the machinery, the early rising, the half-hour dinner, and so on?"

I saw that my discontented friend was not in a humour to give me an answer—and I therefore went on with my talk.

"You are fully aware, Ellen, that a country life does not exclude people from labor—to say nothing of the inferior privileges of attending public worship—that people have often to go a distance to meeting of any kind—that books cannot be so easily obtained as they can here—that you cannot always have just such a society as you wish—that you"—

She interrupted me, by saying, "We have no bell, with its everlasting ding-dong."

"What difference does it make," said I, "whether you shall be awaked by a bell, or the noisy bustle of a farmhouse? For, you know, farmers are generally up as early in the morning as we are obliged to rise. "

"But then, " said Ellen, "country people have none of the clattering of machinery constantly dinning in their ears."

"True," I replied, "but they have what is worse-and that is, a dull, lifeless silence around them. The hens may cackle sometimes, and the geese gabble, and the pigs squeal"—

Ellen's hearty laugh interrupted my description—and presently we proceeded, very pleasantly, to compare a country life with a factory life in Lowell. Her scowl of discontent had departed, and she was prepared to consider the subject candidly. We agreed, that since we must work for a living, the mill, all things considered, is the most pleasant, and best calculated to promote our welfare; that we will work diligently during the hours of labor; improve our leisure to the best advantage, in the cultivation of the mind,—hoping thereby not only to increase our own pleasure, but also to add to the happiness of those around us.

ALMIRA

"A Second Peep at Factory Life"

Source: Josephine L. Baker, *Lowell Offering*, Volume V, 1845, pp. 99-100.

...You ask, if there are so many things objectionable, why we work in the mill. Well, simply for this reason,—every situation in life, has its trials which must be borne, and factory life has no more than any other. There are many things we do not like; many occurrences that send the warm blood mantling to the cheek when they must be borne in silence, and many harsh words and acts that are not called for. There are objections also to the number of hours we work, to the length of time allotted to our meals, and to the low wages allowed for labor; objections that must and will be answered; for the time has come when something, besides the clothing and feeding of the body is to be thought of; when the mind is to be clothed and fed; and this cannot be as it should be, with the present system of labor. Who, let me ask, can find that pleasure in life which they should, when it is spent in this way. Without time for the laborer's own work, and the improvement of the mind, save the few evening hours; and even then if the mind is enriched and stored with useful knowledge, it must be at the expense of health. And the feeling too, that comes over us (there is no use in denying it) when we hear the bell calling us away from repose that tired nature loudly claims—the feeling, that we are *obliged to go*. And these few hours, of which we have spoken, are far too short, three at the most at the close of day. Surely, methinks, every heart that lays claim to humanity will feel 'tis not enough. But this, we hope will, ere long, be done away with, and labor made what it should be; pleasant and inviting to every son and daughter of the human family.

There is a brighter side to this picture, over which we would not willingly pass without notice, and an answer to the question, why we work here? The time we *do* have is our own. The money we earn comes promptly; more so than in any other situation; and our work, though laborious is the same from day to day; we know what it is, and when finished we feel perfectly free, till it is time to commence it again.

New England Factory Life – Bell Time, *Harper's Weekly*, vol. 12 *(July 25, 1868), engraving from a drawing by Winslow Homer.*

Account of Charles Dickens

Source: Charles Dickens, *American Notes* (1842) (reprinted New York: St. Martin's Press, 1985), pp. 60-63.

I happened to arrive at the first factory just as the dinner hour was over, and the girls were returning to their work; indeed, the stairs of the mill were thronged with them as I ascended. These girls...were all well dressed: and that phrase necessarily includes extreme cleanliness....They were healthy in appearance, many of them remarkably so, and had the manners and deportment of young women: not degraded brutes of burden....

The rooms in which they worked, were as well ordered as themselves. In the windows of some, there were green plants, which were trained to shade the glass; in all, there was as much fresh air, cleanliness, and comfort as the nature of the occupation would possibly admit of. Out of so large a number of females, many of whom were only then just verging upon womanhood, it may be reasonably supposed that some were delicate and fragile in appearance: no doubt there were. But I solemnly declare, that from all the crowd I saw in the different factories that day, I cannot recall or separate one young face that gave me a painful impression; not one young girl whom, assuming it to be matter of necessity that she should gain her daily bread by the labour of her hands, I would have removed from those works if I had had the power.

They reside in various boarding-houses near at hand. The owners of the mills are particularly careful to allow no person to enter upon the possession of these houses, whose characters have not undergone the most searching and thorough inquiry. Any complaint that is made against them by the boarders, or by any one else, is fully investigated; and if good ground for complaint be shown to exist against them, they are removed, and their occupation is handed over to some more deserving person. There are a few children employed in these factories, but not many. The laws of the State forbid their working more than nine months in the year, and require that they be educated during the other three. For this purpose there are schools in Lowell; and there are churches and chapels of various persuasions, in which the young women may observe that form of worship in which they have been educated.

At some distance from the factories, and on the highest and pleasantest ground in the neighbourhood, stands their hospital, or boarding-house for the sick: it is the best house in those parts, and was built by an eminent merchant for his own residence. Like that institution at Boston, which I have before described, it is not parcelled out into wards, but is divided into convenient chambers, each of which has all the comforts of a very comfortable home. The principal medical attendant resides under the same roof; and were the patients members of his own family, they could not be better cared for, or attended with greater gentleness and consideration. The weekly charge in this establishment for each female patient is three dollars, or twelve shillings English; but no girl employed by any of the corporations is ever excluded for want of the means of payment. That they do not very often want the means may be gathered from the fact, that in July, 1841, no fewer than nine hundred and seventy-eight of these girls were depositors in the Lowell Savings Bank: the amount of whose joint savings was estimated at one hundred thousand dollars, or twenty thousand English pounds.

I am now going to state three facts, which will startle a large class of readers on this side of the Atlantic very much.

Firstly, there is a joint-stock piano in a great many of the boarding-houses. Secondly, nearly all these young ladies subscribe to circulating libraries. Thirdly, they have got up among themselves a periodical called THE LOWELL OFFERING, "a repository of original articles, written exclusively by females actively employed in the mills,"— which is duly printed, published, and sold; and whereof I brought away from Lowell four hundred good solid pages, which I have read from beginning to end.

The large class of readers, startled by these facts, will exclaim, with one voice, "How very preposterous!" On my deferentially inquiring why, they will answer, "These things are above their station." In reply to that objection, I would beg to ask what their station is.

It is their station to work. And they *do* work. They labour in these mills, upon an average, twelve hours a day, which is unquestionably work, and pretty tight work too. Perhaps it is above their station to indulge in such amusements on any terms. Are we quite sure that we in England have not formed our ideas of the "station" of working-people, from accustoming ourselves to the contemplation of that class as they are, and not as they might be? I think that if we examine our own feelings, we shall find that the pianos, and the circulating libraries, and even the Lowell Offering, startle us by their novelty, and not by their bearing upon any abstract question of right or wrong.

...Of the merits of the Lowell Offering as a literary production I will only observe, putting entirely out of sight the fact of the articles having been written by these girls after the arduous labours of the day, that it will compare advantageously with a great many English Annuals. It is pleasant to find that many of its Tales are of the Mills, and of those who work in them; that they inculcate habits of self-denial and contentment, and teach good doctrines of enlarged benevolence. A strong feeling for the beauties of nature, as displayed in the solitudes the writers have left at home, breathes through its pages like wholesome village air, and though a circulating library is a favourable school for the study of such topics, it has very scant allusion to fine clothes, fine marriages, fine houses, or fine life....

...In this brief account of Lowell,...I have carefully abstained from drawing a comparison between these factories and those of our own land. Many of the circumstances whose strong influence has been at work for years in our manufacturing towns have not arisen here; and there is no manufacturing population in Lowell, so to speak: for these girls (often the daughters of small farmers) come from other States, remain a few years in the mills, and then go home for good.

The contrast would be a strong one, for it would be between the Good and Evil, the living light and deepest shadow. I abstain from it, because I deem it just to do so. But I only the more earnestly adjure all those whose eyes may rest on these pages, to pause and reflect upon the difference between this town and those great haunts of desperate misery: to call to mind, if they can in the midst of party strife and squabble, the efforts that must be made to purge them of their suffering and danger: and last, and foremost, to remember how the precious Time is rushing by.

A Response to Mr. Dickens from the Lowell Offering

Source: Editorial, *Lowell Offering*, Volume III, 1843, pp. 95-96.

...We trust that we feel grateful for his [Charles Dickens'] kindness, and proud of his approval; but we fear that we do not deserve all his commendaton, that we are not worthy of such flattering compliments. He says, "Firstly, there is a piano in a great many of the boarding-houses." That is true, but not in a great proportion of them. "Secondly, nearly all these young ladies subscribe to Circulating Libraries." We fear that *nearly* all do not thus subscribe, though very many are supporters of other libraries. "Thirdly, they have got up, among themselves, a periodical called THE LOWELL OFFERING." The Offering was got up by individuals from *among themselves*, and they perhaps are worthy of our author's applause, but the proportion of those factory girls who interest themselves in its support is not more than one in fifty. Still it is right that all should share the credit, if the general rule is a just one, to judge of a body by their prominent individuals.

"The City of a Day"

Source: John Greenleaf Whittier, *The Prose Works of John Greenleaf Whittier* (Boston: Houghton, Mifflin and Company, 1892), Vol. I, pp. 351-355.

The poet John Greenleaf Whittier wrote in 1843 about Lowell, in this piece entitled "The City of a Day."

This, then, is Lowell, -- a city springing up, like the enchanted palaces of the Arabian tales, as it were in a single night, stretching far and wide its chaos of brick masonry and painted shingles, filling the angle of the confluence of the Concord and the Merrimac with the sights and sounds of trade and industry. Marvellously here have art and labor wrought their modern miracles. I can scarcely realize the fact that a few years ago these rivers, now tamed and subdued to the purposes of man and charmed into slavish subjection to the wizard of mechanism, rolled unchecked towards the ocean the waters of the Winnipesaukee and the rock-rimmed springs of the White Mountains, and rippled down their falls in the wild freedom of Nature. A stranger, in view of all this wonderful change, feels himself, as it were, thrust forward into a new century; he seems treading on the outer circle of the millennium of steam engines and cotton mills. Work is here the patron saint. Everything bears his image and superscription. Here is no place for that respectable class of citizens called gentlemen, and their much vilified brethren, familiarly known as loafers. Over the gateways of this new world Manchester glares the inscription, "Work, or die!"...

...for this is indeed a city consecrated to thrift,-- dedicated, every square rod of it, to the divinity of work; the gospel of industry preached daily and hourly from some thirty temples, each huger than the Milan Cathedral or the Temple of Jeddo, the Mosque of St. Sophia or the Chinese pagoda of a hundred bells; its mighty sermons uttered by steam and water-power; its music the everlasting jar of mechanism and the organ-swell of many waters; scattering the cotton and woollen leaves of its evangel from the wings of steamboats and rail-cars throughout the land; its thousand priests and its thousands of priestesses ministering around their spinning-jenny and powerloom altars, or thronging the long, unshaded streets in the level light of sunset. After all, it may well be questioned whether this gospel, according to Poor Richard's Almanac, is precisely calculated for the redemption of humanity. Labor, graduated to man's simple wants, necessities, and unperverted tastes, is doubtless well; but all beyond this is weariness to flesh and spirit. Every web which falls from these restless looms has a history more or less connected with sin and suffering, beginning with slavery and ending with overwork and premature death.

Many of the streets of Lowell present a lively and neat aspect, and are adorned with handsome public and private buildings; but they lack one pleasant feature of older towns,--broad, spreading shade-trees. One feels disposed to quarrel with the characteristic utilitarianism of the first settlers, which swept so entirely away the green beauty of Nature. For the last few days it has been as hot here as Nebuchadnezzar's furnace or Monsieur Chabert's oven, the sun glaring down from a copper sky upon these naked, treeless streets, in traversing which one is tempted to adopt the language of a warm-weather poet:

> "The lean, like walking skeletons, go stalking pale
>   and gloomy;
> The fat, like redhot warming-pans, send hotter fancies
>   through me;
> I wake from dreams of polar ice, on which I've been
>   a slider,
> Like fishes dreaming of the sea and waking in the spider."

How unlike the elm-lined avenues of New Haven, upon whose cool and graceful panorama the stranger looks down upon the Judge's Cave, or the vine-hung pinnacles of West Rock, its tall spires rising white and clear above the level greenness!-- or the breezy leafiness of Portland, with its wooded islands in the distance, and itself overhung with verdant beauty, rippling and waving in the same cool breeze which stirs the waters of the beautiful Bay of Casco! But time will remedy all this; and, when Lowell shall have numbered half the years of her sister cities, her newly planted elms and maples, which now only cause us to contrast their shadeless stems with the leafy glory of their parents of the forest, will stretch out to the future visitor arms of welcome and repose.

Further Descriptions of Factory Life

Source: *Boston Daily Evening Voice*, February 28, 1867.

To the Editor of the Daily Evening Voice:

Thirty years ago I was a factory girl in the city of Lowell. I was ambitious to do something for myself in the way of earning money to pay my expenses at an Academy; and being too young to teach school in the country, not strong enough to do housework or learn a trade, I went into the card-room on the Fremont Corporation. My work was easy; I could sit down part of the time, and received ($1.75) one dollar and seventy-five cents per week beside my board. Being fond of reverie, and in the habit of constructing scenes and building castles in the air, I enjoyed factory life very well.

After a few months my parents removed from a country town to Lowell, and I went to board with them on the street, and then I began seriously to reflect on the realities of life.

For a delicate girl of fourteen years of age to be called out of bed and be obliged to eat her breakfast without any light, and then frequently wallow through the snow to the factory, stay there until half-past twelve, then run home and swallow her dinner without mastication, run back and stay there until half-past seven, is, to say the least, very unpleasant and unnatural, and exceedingly hurtful to the constitution.

I attended school three months during the following summer; then worked about eighteen months longer in the factory; afterwards worked in the weave-room, in all three years, but only about six months at a time, as my health would not allow me to work longer. The labor of attending three or four looms thirteen hours per day, with no time for recreation or mental improvement is very severe.

The habit of standing on the feet frequently produces varicose veins; and though the girls seldom complain, for they know it is useless, yet it is a fact that factory girls are great sufferers in this respect.

In those days the morals of the girls were well guarded, and they were generally treated respectfully by the overseers, and I think lived well on the corporations.

They were generally daughters of our New England farmers and mechanics, some of them were well educated. Many of them had learned trades. Some of them were of a literary turn and got up improvement circles. And I will say in truth that if the hours of labor had been only eight instead of thirteen, I should prefer working in the mill to house work, enjoyed the society of the girls, and the noise of the machinery was not displeasing to me; but after one has worked from daylight until dark, the prospect of working two or three hours more by lamp light is very discouraging.

In 1849 I was thrown into the society of several young women who were daughters of mill owners; and the contrast between their condition and that of the operatives was so great that it led me to serious reflection on the injustice of society. These girls had an abundance of leisure, could attend school when and where they pleased, were fashionably dressed, were not obliged to work any except when they pleased; indeed, they suffered for want of exercise;

and while they were so tenderly cared for, lest the "winds of heaven should visit their faces too roughly," the operatives toiled on through summer's heat and winter's cold; many passing into an early grave in consequence of protracted labor, and many others making themselves invalids for life.

For one, I could never see the justice of one set of girls working all the time in order that another set should live in ease and idleness. Cowper says, "I would not have a slave to till my ground, to fan me while I sleep, and tremble when I wake, for all the wealth that sinews bought and sold have ever earned." But many of our people in Massachusetts are quite willing to make fat dividends on the labor of anybody they can hire, widows and orphans, boys and girls of tender age; and when they cannot obtain American girls, they send across the ocean for operatives, and then allow them just enough to keep them from starvation.

I am satisfied from my own experience, as well as from observation of the working classes for many years, that nothing can be done for their education or elevation, until the hours of labor are reduced. After one has worked from ten to fourteen hours at manual labor, it is impossible to study History, Philosophy, or Science.

I well remember the chagrin I often felt when attending lectures, to find myself unable to keep awake; or perhaps so far from the speaker on account of being late, that the ringing in my ears caused by the noise of the looms during the day, prevented my hearing scarcely a sentence he uttered. I am sure few possessed a more ardent desire for knowledge than I did, but such was the effect of the long hour system, that my chief delight was, after the evening meal, to place my aching feet in any easy position, and read a novel. I was never too tired, however, to listen to the lectures given by the friends of Labor Reform, such as John Allen, John C. Cluer, or Mike Walsh. I assisted in getting signers to a Ten Hour petitions [sic] to the Legislature, and since I have resided in Boston and vicinity have seen and enjoyed the good results of the improvement in the condition of the working classes.

A WORKING WOMAN

Lucy Larcom began work as a mill worker, later took a bookkeeping position in the Lawrence Mills, and then returned to mill work. She wrote about the physical demands involved in handling the machinery required in her new mill job:

My return to mill-work involved making acquaintance with a new kind of machinery. The spinning-room was the only I had hitherto known anything about. Now my sister Emilie found a place for me in the dressing-room, beside herself. It was more airy, and fewer girls were in the room, for the dressing-frame itself was a large, clumsy affair, that occupied a great deal of space. Mine seemed to me an unmanageable as an overgrown spoilt child. It had to be watched in a dozen directions every minute, and even then it was always getting itself and me into trouble. I felt as if the half-live creature, with its great, groaning joints and whizzing fan, was aware of my incapacity to manage it, and had a fiendish spite against me. I contracted an unconquerable dislike to it; indeed, I had never liked, and never could learn to like, any kind of machinery. And this machine finally conquered me. It was humiliating, but I had to acknowledge that there were some things I could not do, and I retired from the field, vanquished.

Source: Larcom, *A New England Girlhood*, p. 226.

75 Young Women

From 15 to 35 Years of Age,

WANTED TO WORK IN THE

COTTON MILLS!

IN LOWELL AND CHICOPEE, MASS.

I am authorized by the Agents of said Mills to make the following proposition to persons suitable for their work, viz:—They will be paid $1.00 per week, and board, for the first month It is presumed they will then be able to go to work at job prices. They will be considered as engaged for one year, cases of sickness excepted I will pay the expenses of those who have not the means to pay for themselves and the girls will pay it to the Company by their first labor. All that remain in the employ of the Company eighteen months will have the amount of their expenses to the Mills refunded to them. They will be properly cared for in sickness. It is hoped that none will go except those whose circumstances will admit of their staying at least one year. None but active and healthy girls will be engaged for this work as it would not be advisable for either the girls or the Company.

I shall be at the Howard Hotel, Burlington, on Monday, July 25th; at Farnham's, St Albans, Tuesday forenoon, 26th, at Keyse's, Swanton, in the afternoon; at the Massachusetts' House, Rouses Point, on Wednesday, the 27th, to engage girls,---such as would like a place in the Mills would do well to improve the present opportunity, as new hands will not be wanted late in the season. I shall start with my Company, for the Mills, on Friday morning, the 29th inst., from Rouses Point, at 6 o'clock. Such as do not have an opportunity to see me at the above places, can take the cars and go with me the same as though I had engaged them.

I will be responsible for the safety of all baggage that is marked in care of I. M. BOYNTON, and delivered to my charge.

I. M. BOYNTON,

Agent for Procuring Help for the Mills.

Early Labor Unrest

Source: Robinson, *Loom and Spindle*, pp. 51.

One of the first strikes of cotton-factory operatives that ever took place in this country was that in Lowell, in October, 1836. When it was announced that the wages were to be cut down, great indignation was felt, and it was decided to strike, *en masse*. This was done. The mills were shut down, and the girls went in procession from their several corporations to the "grove" on Chapel Hill, and listened to "incendiary" speeches from early labor reformers.

One of the girls stood on a pump, and gave vent to the feelings of her companions in a neat speech, declaring that it was their duty to resist all attempts at cutting down the wages. This was the first time a woman had spoken in public in Lowell, and the event caused surprise and consternation among her audience.

Cutting down the wages was not their only grievance, nor the only cause of this strike. Hitherto the corporations had paid twenty-five cents a week towards the board of each operative, and now it was their purpose to have the girls pay the sum; and this, in addition to the cut in wages, would make a difference of at least one dollar a week. It was estimated that as many as twelve or fifteen hundred girls turned out, and walked in procession though the streets. They had neither flags nor music, but sang songs, a favorite (but rather inappropriate) one being a parody on "I won't be a nun."

> "Oh! isn't it a pity, such a pretty girl as I—
> Should be sent to the factory to pine away and die?
> Oh! I cannot be a slave,
> I will not be a slave,
> For I'm so fond of liberty
> That I cannot be a slave."

My own recollection of this first strike (or "turn out" as it was called) is very vivid. I worked in a lower room, where I had heard the proposed strike fully, if not vehemently, discussed; I had been an ardent listener to what was said against this attempt at "oppression" on the part of the corporation, and naturally I took sides with the strikers. When the day came on which the girls were to turn out, those in the upper rooms started first, and so many of them left that our mill was at once shut down. Then, when the girls in my room stood irresolute, uncertain what to do, asking each other, "Would you?" or "Shall we turn out?" and not one of them having the courage to lead off, I, who began to think they would not go out, after all their talk, became impatient, and started on ahead, saying, with childish bravado, "I don't care what you do, I am going to turn out, whether anyone else does or not;" and I marched out, and was followed by the others. [In a footnote to the text, Mrs. Robinson states: "I was then eleven years and eight months old."]

As I looked back at the long line that followed me, I was more proud than I have ever been since at any success I may have achieved, and more proud than I shall be again until my own beloved State gives to its women citizens the right of suffrage.

The agent of the corporation where I then worked took some small revenges on the supposed ringleaders; on the principle of sending the weaker to the wall, my mother was turned away from her boarding-house, that functionary saying, "Mrs. Hanson, you could not prevent the older girls from turning out, but your daughter is a child, and *her* you could control."

It is hardly necessary to say that so far as results were concerned this strike did no good. The dissatisfaction of the operatives subsided, or burned itself out, and though the authorities did not accede to their demands, the majority returned to their work, and the corporation went on cutting down the wages.

And after a time, as the wages became more and more reduced, the best portion of the girls left and went to their homes, or to the other employments that were fast opening to women, until there were very few of the old guard left; and thus the *status* of the factory population of New England gradually became what we know it to be to-day.

Female Labor Reform Association, *Voice of Industry,* and *Factory Tracts*

Source: *Voice of Industry,* November 7, 1845.

The first female factory workers' unions were organized in different cities under the Female Labor Reform Association, and Lowell mill workers established the Lowell Female Labor Reform Association in January 1845.

Among other activities, the Lowell Female Labor Reform Association published in 1845 "Factory Tracts," an exposition of factory life written by mill workers.

Voice of Industry, a labor newspaper begun in 1845 and published first in Fitchburg, Massachusetts and later in Lowell, was acquired by the Lowell Female Labor Reform Association.

"Factory Life As It Is, by an Operative"

Source: *Factory Tracts, Number One*, October 1845.

...Much has been written and spoken in woman's behalf, especially in America; and yet a large class of females are, and have been, destined to a state of servitude as degrading as unceasing toil can make it. I refer to the female operatives of New England—the *free* states of our union—the boasted land of equal rights for all—the states where no colored slave can breathe the balmy air, and exist as such;—but yet there are those, a host of them, too, who are in fact nothing more nor less than slaves in every sense of the word! Slaves to a system of labor which requires them to toil from five until seven o'clock, with one hour only to attend to the wants of nature, allowed—slaves to the will

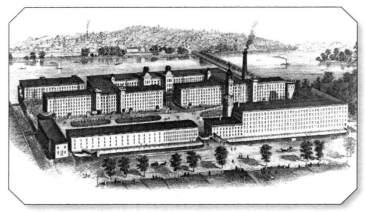

Boott Cotton Mills, engraving 1880 (Courtesy Lowell National Historic Park)

and requirements of the "powers that be," however they may infringe on the rights or conflict with the feelings of the operative—slaves to ignorance—and how can it be otherwise? What time has the operative to bestow on moral, religious or intellectual culture? How can our country look for naught but ignorance and vice, under the existing state of things? When the whole system is exhausted by unremitting labor during twelve and thirteen hours per day, can any reasonable being expect that the mind will retain its vigor and energy? Impossible! Common sense will teach every one the utter impossibility of improving the mind under these circumstances, however great the desire may be for knowledge....

AN OPERATIVE

"The Evils of Factory Life"

Source: *Factory Tracts, Number One*, October 1845.

Among the first which we shall notice, is the tendency it [factory life] has, at the present time, to destroy all love of order and practice in domestic affairs. It is a common remark, that by the time a young lady has worked in a factory one year, she will lose all relish for the quiet, fireside comforts of life, and the neatness attendant upon order and precision. The truth is, time is wanting, and opportunity, in order to cultivate the mind and form good habits. All is hurry, bustle and confusion in the street, in the mill, and in the overflowing boarding house. If there chance to be an intelligent mind in that crowd which is striving to lay up treasures of knowledge, how unfavorably is it situated! Crowded into a small room which contains three beds and six females, all possessing the "without end" tongue of woman, what chance is there for *studying?* and much less for sober thinking and reflecting? Some lofty, original minds, we will allow, have surmounted all the obstacles of a factory life and come out, like gold, refined from all the dross of baneful society and pernicious examples, but they are cases of rare occurrence. But few have the moral courage and perseverance to travel on in the rugged paths of science and improvement, amid all these and many other discouragements. After thirteen hours unremitting toil, day after day and week after week, how much energy and life would remain to nerve on the once vigorous mind in the path of wisdom? What ambition or pride would such females possess, to enable them to practice good order and neatness! They are confined so long in close, unhealthy rooms that it is a greater wonder that they possess any life or animation, more than the machines which they have watched so unceasingly!

Let us look forward into the future, and what does the picture present to our imagination! Methinks I behold the self same females occupying new and responsible stations in society. They are now wives and mothers! But oh! how deficient in everything pertaining to those holy, *sacred* names! Behold what disorder, confusion and disquietude reigns, where quiet, neatness and calm serenity should sanctify and render almost like heaven the home of domestic union and love! Instead of being qualified to rear a family—to instruct them in the great duties of life—to cultivate and unfold the intellect—to imbue the soul in the true and living principles of right and justice—to teach them the most important of all lessons, the art of being *useful* members in the world, ornaments in society and blessings to all around them,—*they*, themselves, have need to be instructed in the *very first principles* of living well and thinking right. Incarcerated within the walls of a factory, while as yet mere children—drilled there from five till seven o'clock, year after year—thrown into company with all sorts and descriptions of minds, dispositions and intellects, without counsellor or friend to advise—far away from a watchful mother's tender care, or father's kind instruction—surrounded on all sides with the vain ostentation of fashion, vanity and light frivolity—beset with temptations without, and the carnal propensies of nature within, what *must*, what *will* be the natural, rational result? What but ignorance, misery, and *premature decay* of both *body* and *intellect?* Our country will be but one great hospital, filled with worn out operatives and colored slaves! Those who marry, even, become a curse instead of a help-meet to their husbands, because of having broken the laws of God and their own physical natures, in these modern prisons (alias palaces,) in the gardens of Eden! It has been remarked by some writer that the mother educates the man. Now, if this be a truth, as we believe it is, to a very great extent what, we would ask, are we to expect, the same system of labor prevailing, will be the mental and intellectual character of the future generations of New England? What but a race weak, sickly, imbecile, both mental and physical? A race fit only for coporation tools and time-serving slaves? Nobility of America!—producers of all the luxuries and comforts of life! will you not *wake up* on this subject? Will you sit supinely down and let the drones in society fasten the yoke of tyranny, which is already fitted to your necks so cunningly that you do not feel it but slightly,—will you, I say suffer them to rivet that yoke upon you, which has crushed and is crushing its millions in the old world to earth; yea, to starvation and death? Now is the time to answer this all-important question. Shall we not hear the response from every hill and vale, "EQUAL RIGHTS, or death to the corporations"? God grant it is the fervent prayer of

JULIANNA.

Lowell, October, 1845.

"Some of the Beauties of Our Factory System. . .Otherwise, Lowell Slavery"

by Amelia [Sargent]

Source: *Factory Tracts, Number One*, October 1845.

Amelia Sargent submitted the following article first to the Lowell Offering, where it was rejected by editor Harriet Farley, and then to the Female Labor Reform Association. It was published with both submission letters, and the letter to the Female Labor Reform Association mentioned the rejection of the article by the Lowell Offering.

For the purpose of illustration, let us go with that light-hearted, joyous young girl who is about for the first time to leave the home of her childhood, that home around which clusters so many beautiful and holy associations, pleasant memories, and quiet joys; to leave, too, a mother's cheerful smile, a father's care and protection; and wend her way toward this far famed "city of spindles," this promised land of the imagination, in whose praise she has doubtless heard so much.

Let us trace her progress during her first year's residence, and see whether she indeed realizes those golden prospects which have been held out to her. Follow her now as she enters that large gloomy looking building— she is in search of employment, and has been told that she might here obtain an eligible situation. She is sadly wearied with her journey, and withal somewhat annoyed by the noise, confusion, and strange faces all around her. So, after a brief conversation with the overseer, she concludes to accept the first situation which offers; and reserving to herself a sufficient portion of time in which to obtain the necessary rest after her unwonted exertions, and the gratification of a stranger's curiosity regarding the place in which she is now to make her future home, she retires to her boarding-house, to arrange matters as much to her mind as may be.

The intervening time passes rapidly away, and she soon finds herself once more within the confines of that close noisy apartment, and is forthwith installed in her new situation—first, however, premising that she has been sent to the Counting-room, and receives therefrom a Regulation paper, containing the rules by which she must be governed while in their employ; and lo! here is the beginning of mischief; for in addition to the tyrannous and oppressive rules which meet her astonished eyes, she finds herself compelled to remain for the space of twelve months in the very place she then occupies, however reasonable and just cause of complaint might be hers, or however strong the wish for dismission; thus, in fact, constituting herself a slave, a very slave to the caprices of him for whom she labors...

...the next beautiful feature which she discovers in this *glorious* system is the long number of hours which she is obliged to spend in the above named close, unwholesome apartment. It is not enough, that like the poor peasant of Ireland, or the Russian serf who labors from sun to sun, but during one half of the year, she must still continue to toil on, long after Nature's lamp has ceased to lend its aid—nor will even this suffice to satisfy the grasping avarice of her employer; for she is also through the winter months required to rise, partake of her morning meal, and be at her station in the mill, while the sun is yet sleeping behind the eastern hills; thus working on an average, at least twelve hours and three fourths per day, exclusive of the time allotted for her hasty meals, which is in winter simply one half hour at noon,—in the spring is allowed the same at morn, and during the summer is added 15 minutes to the half hour at noon. Then too, when she is at last released from her wearisome day's toil, still may she not depart in peace. No! her footsteps must be dogged to see that they do not stray beyond the corporation limits, and she *must,* whether she will or no, be subjected to the manifold inconveniences of a large crowded boarding-house, where too, the price paid for her accommodation is so utterly insignificant, that it will not ensure to her the common comforts of life; she is obliged to sleep in a small comfortless, half ventilated apartment containing some half a dozen occupants each; but no matter, *she is an operative*—it is all well enough for her; there is no "abuse" about it; no, indeed; so think our employers,—but do we think so? time will show.

...Reader will you pronounce this a mere fancy sketch written for the sake of effect? It is not so. It is a real picture of "Factory life;" nor is it one half so bad as might truthfully and justly have been drawn. But it has been asked, and doubtless will be again, why, if these evils are so aggravating, have they been so long and so peacefully borne? Ah! and why have they? It is a question well worthy of our consideration, and we would call upon every operative in *our* city, aye, throughout the length and breadth of the land, to awake from the lethargy which has fallen upon them, and assert and maintain their rights. We call upon you for action—*united and immediate action.* But, says one, let us wait till we are stronger. In the language of one of old, we ask, when shall we be stronger? Will it be the next week, or the next year? Will it be when we are reduced to the servile condition of the poor operatives of England? for verily we shall be and that right soon if matters be suffered to remain as they are. Says another, how shall we act? we are but one amongst a thousand, what shall we do that our influence may be felt in this vast multitude? We answer, there is in this city an Association called the Female Labor Reform Association, having for its professed object, the amelioration of the condition of the operative. Enrolled up on its records are the names of five hundred members— come then, and add thereto five hundred or rather five thousand more, and in the strength of our united influence we will soon show these *drivelling* cotton lords, this mushroom aristocracy of New England, who so arrogantly aspire to lord it over God's heritage, that our rights cannot be trampled upon with impunity; that we will no longer submit to that arbitrary power which has for the last ten years been so abundantly exercised over us. One word ere we close, to the hardy independent yeomanry and mechanics, among the Granite Hills of New Hampshire, the woody forests of Maine, the cloud capped mountains of Vermont, and the busy, bustling towns of the old Bay State—ye! who have daughters and sisters toiling in these sickly prison-houses which are scattered far and wide over each of these States, we appeal to *you* for aid in this matter. Do you ask how that aid can be administered? We answer through the Ballot Box. Yes! if you have one spark of sympathy for our condition, carry it there, and see to it that you send to preside in the Councils of each Commonwealth, men who have hearts as well as heads, souls as well bodies; men who will watch zealously over the interests of the laborer in every department; who will protect him by the strong arm of the law from the encroachments of arbitrary power; who will see that he is not deprived of those rights and privileges which God and Nature have bestowed upon him—yes,

> From every rolling river,
> From mountain, vale and plain,
> We call on you to deliver
> Us, from the tyrant's chain:
> And shall we call in vain? we trust not. More anon.
>
> AMELIA.

Extract from *Factory Tracts, Number 2*

Source: *Voice of Industry*, November 14, 1845.

The Voice of Industry published the following excerpts from the Female Labor Reform Association's second volume of its Factory Tracts:

The subject of factory labor and the regulations by which the operatives are governed, is a subject in which our country is ignorant. By our country I do not mean New Orleans and Texas *alone*, but will include Massachusetts. It is not unusual to hear a citizen of Boston, Salem, or Lynn, inquire about our regulations, and express their surprise of them.

I would not be understood as contending against system, or good regulations, I believe them to be for the good of all concerned—but when they conflict with our rights as rational beings, and we are regarded as living machines, and all the rules made subservient to the interest of the employer; then it would seem that we have a right to call them in question, and regard them as arbitrary, and call for a reform.

I refer particularly to the rule which compels all who work for the companies, to board in their houses. There has been some difference of opinion, or of words on this regulation. Some contend that it is no "abuse" of power to compel the Operatives to leave the quiet fireside of a friend and board with the mixed multitude congregated in a large boarding house. Others think that the time and labor *only,* are bought by the employers, and the Operative has no right to be dictated as it regards the duties he owes to himself or those of his friends, providing they do not interfere with the duty he owes to his or her employer.

We are told by those who contend for corporated rules, that the Operatives of Lowell, are the virtuous daughters of New England. If this be true, (and we believe it is with few exceptions,) is it necessary to shut them up at night, six in a room, 14 by 16 feet with all the trunks, and boxes necessary to their convenience; to keep them so? Are they not qualified to procure a place for themselves, that suits their own taste or convenience? — have they no judgement of their own that this interference is made? Is it not a violation of our principles of christianity, which says: — "as we would that others should do unto you, do ye even so unto them," and we think that every superintendent of Lowell would justify us in saying that they would think themselves grossly insulted if the directors of the companies should make and enforce such rules for them, as they make for others.

Such kind reader, are the accommodations for improvement and cultivation. Those who keep the boarding houses do all in their power in most cases to make the stay of the girls pleasant, and much credit is due to them. But the means are inadequate to meet the wants of the operatives, and too many are made to occupy the same sleeping and sitting apartment.

Another objection to this rule, is the impossibility of personal cleanliness and frequent bathing so necessary to health; it would be expressing a doubt of the good sense of our readers to contend for a sufficient amount of accommodation to allow every girl ample *time* and room to bathe once in each day.

We shall be justified by every physiologist in saying, that every operative who is compelled to room with five others, is thereby compelled to violate the physical laws of God, and so sure as these laws are immutable, so sure disease and premature decay *must* be the consequence.

There may be as many long stories told about the good health of the operatives, and factory labor being so conducive to health and intelligence as would reach from Georgia to Maine, and an intelligent community will not believe them when we tell them the girls are obliged to violate all the laws of health every day, and every night by sleeping, from six to sixteen in a room, and this is no exaggeration.

Philosophy has gained the ascendancy, and the physical laws are regarded as the laws of God, and a strict obedience to them is enforced, and those who would make the world believe that they can be suspended to suit the convenience and interest of the manufacturers, are either grossly stupid or dishonest. I leave the reader to judge in this case.

AN OPERATIVE.

The *Lowell Offering* and *Voice of Industry*

Source: *Voice of Industry*, January 2, 1846.

In an editorial written after the Lowell Offering had ceased publication, the Voice of Industry offered its appraisal of the Lowell Offering:

...Led on by the fatal error of neutrality, it [the Lowell Offering] has neglected the operative as a working being, and to a great degree, under the power of those whose interests are antagonistical; to convince the world that factory girls can write sentimental tales, romantic stories, and poetic rhyme, or in other words, "that there is mind among the spindles."

This the Offering has accomplished, and many articles, both creditable to their authors and the conductors of this magazine, have monthly graced its columns,—but this does not show that *mind was made* "among the spindles," or that factory life, under the present system in conducive to the expansion and cultivation of the intellectual powers of the operatives,—still an influence has gone abroad that the Lowell factories are every way calculated to improve and elevate the moral, mental, and even physical condition, of those who are daily confined from twelve to fourteen [hours] within their walls; and we are sorry to say, that whenever attempts to correct this false impression have been made by those true friends to the operatives and toilers of our country; who have long since discovered an inherent evil in the present organized system of factory labor, which like gangrene is secretly eating away upon the physical and mental constitutions of a large portion of our people; the Offering has forgotten its *neutrality* and taken sides with the oppressor, in denouncing the operative's real friends, as "levelers," "exciters" and "radical meddlers," while it has glossed over and covered up the many gross evils which the factory system is entailing upon society and the world....

In one of the valedictories we find much worthy of admiration, and much to regret,—that, "the injunctions of christianity are not carried into the details of factory life, as they should be," is a truth of significant importance, and worthy a heart that feels for the wrongs and errors of society,—but that, "females who come here, find that they will be respected, if they respect themselves. They will find here lectures, institutes, religious associations and social conventions open to them. They are met and treated according to their worth," evinces a disposition to throw the productive vices and wrongs, engendered by a false social and political organization in society—social and money aristocracy; upon their more unfortunate victims...Of what benefit is it to [a] large portion of the Lowell operatives, that lectures, institutes, and other means of improvement, exist in the city, while they are confined from twelve to fourteen hours in the mills, which paralyzes all relish for mental and social culture? The various institutions of moral, mental and physical improvement, are not "open" to the mass of the factory population, and only those who possess an uncommon thirst for intellectual improvement, accompanied with physical ability, overcome the fatigues of the day and find their way to useful lectures and societies of learning; while multitutdes are only called out by the excitements of mirth and the foolish juggling, of which factory towns are not unfrequently visited. The crowded houses at comic concerts, and clownish performances, and the sparse audience, and empty seats of the lecture room, together with a large amount of vain curiousity which draws people to churches, are strong evidence of the truth of our position. And for this state of things, the false relations of capital and labor are answerable, and those who apologize for, and uphold the present system of factory labor, cannot be considered true friends to human improvement and christian progression.

Agitation for a 10-Hour Day

Source: *Voice of Industry*, December 26, 1845.

Much has been said and written of a very conflicting and unsatisfactory character about the mills of this city, the hours of operation per day and their effect upon the health and condition of the operatives, among which we copy the following:

FACTORY LABOR.—In the reduction of the tariff, among other reasons assigned, will be rapacity of the manufacturers in the severe labor extracted from the girls in the factories. In Lowell, in the shortest days in December, the hours of works are 11.13 minutes; in Nov. 11.46 m.; in January 11.30 m.; in March 11.52 m.; and all the rest of the year 12 hours and ranging from 16 to 55 minutes in addition; and in Manchester, New Hampshire, the lowest is 11 hours 24 minutes, [and] the highest 13 hours! for eight months in the year. This is cruel. Day laborers in the fresh open air only work ten hours, the longest day in the year; in winter only 9 hours. But here are poor, tender girls, in a confined atmosphere, drawing into their lungs the floating fibres of the materials, forced to labor 13 hours in a day—rise in the dark and go to work amidst snow and sleet—and some of them children, and poor and parentless. Our rich manufacturers will not avoid the penny wise and pound foolish system until it is too late.—[N.Y. Sun.

From the tenor of the above extract, we presume it was penned with honest intentions, yet it is incorrect in fact, the time which the mills run, being much longer than represented. Now as our object is to give a fair and impartial statement of all transactions which come under our notice, affecting the interest of the factory operatives, through [which] the people may be enabled to judge correctly of the influences of the present long hour system, upon those who "toil and spin," we introduce a few facts, relative to the hours of factory labor in Lowell.

Upon the Hamilton Corporation, directly opposite our office, Dec. 24th, the operatives are called in and let out the mills at the following periods;

Called in at 20 minutes to 7 A.M., leave for dinner 12 1-2—making	5.50
Called in at 10 minutes before 1 P.M., leave for supper at 7 1-2, making	6.40
Whole time mills operate per day,	12.30

The above is the exact time between the ringing of the bell and the raising and shutting of the gates.

The operatives are allowed ten minutes in morning and ten at noon in going from their boarding houses to the mills, which deducted from the time the wheels are in operation, leaves *twelve hours and ten minutes*, the actual amount of time the operatives are required to labor for day's work, the shortest days in December, exclusive of the time required in going to and from their daily task.

Many who board near the mills, commence work as soon as the gates are raised, consequently make out *twelve and a half* hours of real service during the shortest days in the year.

We are informed by those engaged upon the Middlesex, (Woollen) that the mills on that corporation run still longer, and the goods finding a ready market at great profits, every means is resorted to by the manufacturers to produce the largest possible amount. On no corporation in Lowell, do the mills operate less than twelve hours per day, at this season and in the longest days of Summer they run thus:

Commence in the morning 10 minutes before 5, gates shut down for breakfast, at 7 o'clock, commence again 20 minutes past 7. Gates shut down at half past twelve; commence again 5 minutes past 1; gates shut down for supper at 7; making *thirteen hours and fifteen minutes* between the ringing of the bells, thirty minutes of which is allowed the operatives in going to and from their meals, leaving *twelve hours and forty-five minutes*, of actual service in the mills.

During the month of April, the factories run more hours than in any other month of the year, which is, according to Mr. Miles, thirteen hours and thirty-one minutes. On Saturdays from the 20th of September till about the 20th of March, the operatives are released soon after dark, which will take off upon the average, about one hour per week, during that time.

From the foregoing facts, it will be seen that much deception has been used in reporting the hours of factory labor by self interested men who wish to aggrandize themselves by courting the favor of the manufacturing power of this country. It will be seen, that, at no season of the year, less than twelve hours is considered a regular days work in the Lowell factories and that they range from about twelve hours and ten minutes up to thirteen hours and thirty one minutes, and should the time spent in going to and from the mills be taken into the account, as it ought, the longest days labor, would exceed fourteen and a half hours, and the shortest, never fall below twelve and a half.

We present these few important statistics to the public, as correct, as good intentions, close observation and authentic information will allow, having no disposition to exaggerate or misrepresent, but simply to state things as they *really are*, that our people may come to correct conclusions upon so important a subject, and finally adopt some system of factory labor, more in accordance with the true principles of republican equality and christian justice, which shall secure to the operatives all the blessings of health, plenty and happiness which flow from a life of well directed, virtuous and free industry, instead of dooming them to years of drudgery, want and dependence, making them ready victims to all the physical, mental and moral ills, which poverty, ignorance and overwork are sure to generate.

Petition to Massachusetts Legislature

Source: *Voice of Industry,* January 15, 1845.

We the undersigned peaceable, industrious and hardworking men and women of Lowell, in view of our condition—the evils already come upon us, by toiling from 13 to 14 hours per day, confined in unhealthy apartments, exposed to the poisonous contagion of air, vegetable, animal and mineral properties, debarred from proper Physical Exercise, Mental discipline, and Mastication cruelly limited, and thereby hastening us on through pain, disease and privation, down to a premature grave, pray the legislature to institute a ten-hour working day in all of the factories of the state.

Signed
    John Quincy Adams Thayer
    Sarah G. Bagley
    James Carle
And 2,000 others mostly women

Commonwealth of Massachusetts Report

Source: Massachusetts General Court, House of Representatives, House Documents, No. 50, 1845, pp. 1-6, 15-17.

House of Representatives, March 12, 1845

The Special Committee to which was referred sundry petitions relating to the hours of labor, have considered the same and submit the following REPORT:

The first petition which was referred to your committee, came from the city of Lowell and was signed by Mr. John Quincy Adams Thayer, and eight hundred and fifty others, "peaceable, industrious, hard working men and women of Lowell." The petitioners declare that they are confined to "from thirteen to fourteen hours per day in unhealthy apartments," and are thereby "hastening through pain, disease and privation, down to a premature grave." They therefore ask the Legislature "to pass a law providing that ten hours shall constitute a day's work," and that no corporation or private citizen "shall be allowed, except in cases of emergency, to employ one set of hands more than ten hours per day."

The second petition came from the town of Fall River, and is signed by John Gregory and four hundred and eighty-eight others. These petitions ask for the passage of a law to constitute "ten hours a day's work in *all corporations* created by the Legislature."

...we have come to the conclusion unanimously, that legislation is not necessary at the present time, and for the following reasons:—

1st – That a law limiting the hours of labor, if enacted at all, should be of a general nature. That it should apply to individuals or copartnerships as well as to corporations. Because, if it is wrong to labor more than ten hours in a corporation, it is also wrong when applied to individual employers, and your Committee are not aware that more complaint can justly be made against incorporated companies in regard to the hours of labor, than can be against individuals or copartnerships. But it will be said in reply to this, that corporations are the creatures of the Legislature, and therefore the Legislature can control them in this, as in other matters. This to a certain extent is true, but your Committee go farther than this, and say, that not only are corporations subject to the control of the Legislature but individuals are also, and if it should ever appear that the public morals, the physical condition, or the social well-being of society were endangered, from this cause or from any cause, then it would be in the power and would be the duty of the Legislature to interpose its prerogative to avert the evil.

2nd – Your Committee believe that the factory system, as it is called, is not more injurious to health than other kinds of indoor labor. That a law which would compel all of the factories in Massachusetts to run their machinery but ten hours out of the 24, while those in Maine, New Hampshire, Rhode Island and other States in the union, were not restricted at all, the effect would be the same as closing our mills one day in every week, and although Massachusetts capital, enterprise and industry are willing to compete on fair terms with the same of the other States, and, if needs be, with European nations, yet it is easy to perceive that we could not compete with our sister States, much less with foreign countries, if a restriction of this nature was put upon our manufactories.

3rd – It would be impossible to legislate to restrict the hours of labor, without affecting very materially the question of wages; and that is a matter which experience has taught us can be much better regulated by the parties themselves than by the Legislature. Labor in Massachusetts is a very different commodity from what it is in foreign countries. Here labor is on an equality with capital, and indeed controls it, and so ever will be while free education and free constitutions exist. And although we may find fault, and say, that labor works too many hours, and labor is too severely tasked, yet if we attempt by legislation to enter within its orbit and interfere with its plans, we will be told to keep clear and to mind our own business. Labor is intelligent enough to make its own bargains, and look out for its own interests without any interference from us; and your Committee want no better proof to convince them that Massachusetts men and Massachusetts women, are equal to this, and will take care of themselves better than we can take care of them, than we had from the intelligent and virtuous men and women who appeared in support of this petition, before the Committee.

4th – The Committee do not wish to be understood as conveying the impression, that there are no abuses in the present system of labor; we think there are abuses; we think that many improvements may be made, and we believe will be made, by which labor will not be so severely tasked as it now is. We think that it would be better if the hours for labor were less,—if more time was allowed for meals, if more attention was paid to ventilation and pure air in our manufactories, and work shops, and many other matters. We acknowledge all this, but we say, the remedy is not with us. We look for it in the progressive improvement in art and science, in a higher appreciation of man's destiny, in a less love for money, and a more ardent love for social happiness and intellectual superiority. Your Committee, therefore, while they agree with the petitioners in their desire to lessen the burthens imposed upon labor, differ only as is the means by which these burthens are sought to be removed.

It would be an interesting inquiry were we permitted to enter upon it, to give a brief history of the rise and progress of the factory system in Massachusetts, to speak of its small beginnings, and show its magnificent results. Labor has made it what it is, and labor will continue to improve upon it.

Your Committee, in conclusion, respectfully ask to be discharged from the further consideration of the matters referred to then, and that the petitions be referred to the next General Court.

For the Committee, WM. SCHOULER, Chairman

Wage Slavery

The language of labor agitation drew similarities between Northern factory labor and Southern slavery. The following Voice of Industry editorial reprinted a report from the Strafford Transcript on the petition signed by women in the Lowell mills against the annexation of Texas and resulting extension of slavery within the United States:

A MILE OF GIRLS.—It will be seen, says the Free State Rally, that the women of Lowell, God bless them, who have signed the remonstrance against the extension of slavery, if they were to join hand in hand, would stretch more than a mile. Probably not a few of them are the young women, called "white slaves" at the South, who work in the factories. They have signed the remonstrance from no selfish calculation, but from pure, heaven-inspired sympathy for the oppressed slave.—*Strafford Transcript.*

Yes, "God bless" the factory girls of Lowell—they are a class for whom we entertain no small share of sympathy and esteem and we rejoice to see them enlisted in the great and good cause of emancipating the oppressed slaves of the South.

But while they come up in such a noble phalanx and enter their protest against the nefarious traffic of black slavery, we are led into a train of thought no individuals [sic] who is free to think can shake off, or refrain from expressing if free to speak his honest sentiments.—How comes it that the Lowell factory girls are so *free* to enter their names against the annexation of Texas?...We feel it our duty to question the consistency of that zeal which induces the task-masters of the manufacturing establishments of this city to circulate remonstrances against the extension of black slavery at the South, while thousands of the fair daughters and noble sons of New England, are daily confined from 12 to 14 hours within the prison wall of our noisy, health-destroying and humanity-degrading mills, under their immediate supervision. Why can such articles find free access into the mills, and be urged upon the sympathy of the operatives, while ten hour petitions and every thing calculated to lesson [sic] the hours of labor and ameliorate the condition of those, who have been drawn from the homes of their childhood by pinching necessity, anticipated good or false inducements, to seek empolyment [sic] in the factories, are tyrannically forbidden, and the individual who attempts to offer anything of the kind, is driven from the premises, as a *lawless* intruder? Is not the restoration or God's common blessings, to that important and rapidly increasing portion of our people—the American operatives, the cause of *freedom* and humanity?—

And what is that philanthropy worth, which seeks some object beyond the limits of self-interest, while it neglects, aye fosters the very personification of slavery at home?

...Operatives of Lowell, think of these things and circulate the ten hour petitions throughout every mill and boarding house in the city, and should you receive the opposition of these *circumstantial* philanthropists, meet them on the broad platform of universal justice, and unmask the hypocrisy of those who are perpetuating a system that is depriving you of the common gifts of God, and polluting the altar of Emancipation with the very [sweat] and blood of your existence.

Source: *Voice of Industry,* Lowell, Massachusetts, December 26, 1845.

Letter to the Operatives of Manchester

The Voice of Industry reprinted the following letter from Lowell's Female Labor Reform Association, originally published in the "Manchester Democrat."

Source: *Voice of Industry*, December 24, 1845.

From the Manchester Democrat

LETTER TO THE OPERATIVES OF MANCHESTER
From the Secretary of the
Lowell Female Labor Reform Association.

Sisters in the cause of human improvement and human rights—to your sympathies—to your sense of duty and justice, would we at this time appeal. You have now manifested a good degree of zeal and interest in the work of "Labor Reform," and we hope and trust that you will continue to investigate the subject and take such efficient measures as shall assist in accomplishing the great object of this our noble and philanthropic enterprise, viz:—

The elevation and promotion of the real producers of our country to that station and standing in society which they were by a benificent God designed to occupy. Too long have the virtuous poor been looked down upon as a lower race of beings, while vice and crime of the darkest hue, rolled in luxury and splendor through our streets—too long have our females been treated like as many senseless automatons in the kitchens of the purse-proud aristocrats of our Republic—and as a *part* of the machinery in our manufacturing towns and districts throughout [the] Union. It is now for the working men and working women of these United States to say whether this state of society which debases the masses to a level with the serfs of the old countries shall continue; or whether a new and brighter era shall dawn on the republican shores, giving to all equal rights and true liberty. To effect this glorious work of reform we believe a complete *union* among the worthy toilers and spinners of our own nation so as to have a concert of action, is all that is requisite. By organizing associations and keeping up a correspondence throughout the country and arousing the public mind to a just sense of the claims of humanity, we hope to roll on the great tide of reformation until from every fertile vale and towering hill the response shall be echoed and re-echoed:— *Freedom*—freedom for all!

Operatives of Manchester, you have began [sic] well, may God grant that you persevere united, faithfully, triumphantly! You have now an Association organized and consisting of a goodly number already, and hundreds more are ready to join your ranks, I doubt not, if you prove active and vigilant,—true to yourselves and faithful to the noble enterprise in which you are now engaged. We shall be extremely happy to correspond with you and meet with you in your meetings as often as possible. Let us seek to encourage and strengthen each other in every good word and work.

If discouragements arise as they surely will, will you yield to despair and falter? God forbid! Rather, take the simple motto of your sister Association of Lowell, and let its spirit fire your every heart with NEW ZEAL and unwavering hope—"*We[']ll try again!*" Let us aim in all that we do, to increase the intelligence and knowledge of all—to raise higher the standard of moral and intellectual worth among us—then shall we become stronger and stronger, throwing around us that protecting power which is, and ever will be invincible, the power of knowledge!

...We have now a paper owned and edited in and by our associations, devoted entirely to the Laborer's cause—the cause of humanity and human rights, which it is only necessary to say is emphatically the workmen and women's paper, in order to have every one who feels the least interest in the cause, subscribe for and support....

...In a word, let us be active, firm and united in every good work, until righteousness shall be established throughout the length and breadth of Columbia's land.

Yours until death in the cause of Labor Reform.

Suggested Further Reading

Deitch, JoAnne Weisman, editor. *Children at Work,* 2nd ed. Boston: History Compass, 2006.

Dublin, Thomas, editor. *Farm to Factory: Women's Letters, 1830-1860.* New York: Columbia University Press, 1981.

Dublin, Thomas, editor. *Women at Work.* New York: Columbia University Press, 1979.

Dunwell, S. *The Run of The Mill.* Boston: David R. Godine, Publisher, 1978.

Eno, Arthur L., Jr., editor. *Cotton Was King: A History of Lowell, Massachusetts.* New Hampshire: New Hampshire Publishing Co., 1976.

Foner, Phillip S. *Factory Girl: A Collection of Writings on Life and Struggles in New England Factories of the 1840's.* Urbana, Illinois: University of Illinois Press, 1977.

Josephson, Hannah. *The Golden Threads.* New York: Dueli, Sloane, Pearce, 1949.

Larcom, Lucy. *A New England Girlhood, Outlined from Memory.* Cornerhouse Publishers, Williamstown, MA: 1977.

Mofford, Juliet Haines. *Child Labor in America.* Perspectives on History Series, Carlisle, MA: Discovery Enterprises, Ltd. (History Compass), 1997.

Mofford, Juliet Haines. *Talkin' Union: The American Labor Movement.* Carlisle, MA: Discovery Enterprises, Ltd. (History Compass), 1997.

Robinson, Harriet Hanson. *Loom And Spindle.* Kailua, Hawaii: Press Pacifica, 1976.

Selden, Bernice. *The Mill Girls.* New York: Atheneum, 1983.

Recommended Novels:

Paterson, Katherine. *Lyddie.* Young adults

Zaroulis, Nancy. *Call the Darkness Light.* Older students and adults.

CPSIA information can be obtained at www.ICGtesting.com
Printed in the USA
LVOW10s2024190614

390831LV00030B/897/P